Composition
of a
Woman

Praise for Composition of a Woman

Christine Ray's debut collection 'Composition of a Woman' is an extraordinary glimpse into the essence of what it takes to make, and sometimes simultaneously break, a woman as strikingly powerful as she is beautiful.

Ray brilliantly split 'Composition' into five thoughtful sections that work together beautifully to deliver the maximum impact of each poem while taking the reader deeper into a stunning journey of the mind, the body, the very soul of this person. In 'Composition', Ray reveals so much of what we try to hide, and she does so while dancing between ruthlessly beautiful and heartbreakingly painful.

While Ray's work is often merciless in its unapologetic, in-your-face delivery
the mean girls smelled
like cruelty mixed with uncertainty
disdain peppered with insecurity
ravenous hunger and envy
(What Little Girls Are Made Of)

it is never short of exquisite

*she brings black roses
and moonlight
fireflies like stars in her sky
bare feet caress the dewy ground
night blooming jasmine
reaching up to brush her opal skin*
(Black Roses and Moonlight)

*nor is it ever lacking in white-hot power
I will travel the ancient ways
clothed only in my dark tresses
my alabaster skin
don a crown of rose and poppy
their scent filling the air
I will take back this night
shape its darkness with my hands
make it blaze with stars and moonlight
create a road for my daughters and sisters
to follow home*
(Lilith)

Christine Ray holds nothing back when she writes about the pain of depression and a failing body. She is raw and unashamed when she speaks to sexuality and the way society still reeks of misogyny and the absence of humanity. But at her very best she is empowering, speaking to the brave and reckless women who she lovingly refers to as sisters.

'Composition' is a beautiful book that takes the time to acknowledge that while some of the weight we carry

through life may not be ours to carry, sometimes carrying it is just as important as knowing when to let it all go.
~Nicole Lyons, *The Lithium Chronicles: Volume One*

Some authors compel you to recommend their books to friends. Others you forget relatively quickly. For a book to enter the hallowed halls of a classic almost never happens. 'Composition of a Woman' is such a book. In forty years' time I'll be asking people to read this. I won't pack this book when I move for fear of losing it, I'll put it in my bag. It's a collection that has more than staying power, it's entered our collective consciousness and become one of the books you list alongside other classics and one day I guarantee this book will be listed among the very best poetry written. Though Ray may feel personally trapped by her physical constraints she is actually anything but, through the sheer will of her wordage. If she loses any of her physical grip, she seems to regain that loss in terms of her writing fluency. How do I know? I read poetry for a living, there's indifferent poetry, good poetry, exciting poetry and then there's a poet. The poet breathes and her words become. It's a transformative exercise that appears effortless but is anything but. The poet opens her chest, removes her ribs, reaches in and extracts the very marrow of herself. In this process, she becomes unforgettable. Christine E. Ray is such a poet. Whether discussing Fibromyalgia's egregious hold over her body, her fear of failure, or the determination to feel passion,

Ray's voice is impossible to smother, she's far too stubborn and talented.
Am I biased in my appraisal? If anything, I hold Ray to a higher standard because of what I know of her as a publisher. She's got education, life experience and wicked smarts which when put together creates a literal powerhouse. As a writer she's far less intimidating than she is when she edits and compiles award winning anthologies, she's able to throw herself into the ring, set the glaring lights and say 'go on then, take a look and yes that scares the hell out of me but I'm going to let you anyway.' That's damn gutsy, a little crazy and magnificent all at once. But if she didn't have the gravitas and sheer talent to back up her own poetry, we'd be polite and just nod our heads, we wouldn't lean into her words like they were a drug and breathe deeply. Ray's work has always grasped me tightly around the throat, she holds on, she doesn't let go. Her courage as a writer and the alacrity of her talent leaves me wordless at times, and although she will lament her energies are not what they used to be, she has the creative zeal you rarely see in poets, where despite any set-back she continues to produce high quality astounding work time and again. For every legitimate struggle Ray has experienced, physically or emotionally, and perhaps because of this, she's created a state that is quite the opposite of being numb.

Intensely female, Ray could be the closest to a laurate for females we're going to find in this generation and as such, her ideas, the lengths she goes to express her truth, are breathtaking and never fail to diminish lesser works. That's what you get when you are in the presence of a real talent, someone who blows you away each and every time, seemingly excavating electricity from nothing. If you ever considered a female weak, read a few lines of Ray and you'll soon be corrected. This is so much more than a list of sufferings and experiences; this is the root of womanhood.

Most female writers I know personally wish they had half the originality and momentum Ray has as a creative. Her reach is far, her words are velvet and the allure of her force leaves you vibrating with her presence. If I could buy one collection of poetry for all those I know who love poetry, I'd purchase Ray's work every time. Her passion, focus and willingness to expose the beating meat of her soul, claims her throne as unforgettable and irreplaceable. Realizing control is an illusion Ray has bequeathed us the greater gift, her elemental truth. "When I turned 50 / I was considered obsolete" (Bad Feminist). Fortunately for us, Ray's never been one to listen to small talk.

~Candice Louisa Daquin, *Pinch the Lock*

I sat in bed today and read *Composition of a Woman* from start to finish. I literally could not let go of this book. I savored every damn poem. I tasted her tears; I felt her anguish, her grief, her triumph; I heard Christine Ray's voice *("I am done whispering")*, and it is a beautifully powerful one; it is a voice that will not fade away

anytime soon. Ray has a brilliant ability to weave humor into her poetry, while conveying a powerhouse message. 'Wonder Woman' comes to mind. I've read that poem three times now, and each time I smile a little bit more! Ray's poetry will stick to my ribs and flow through my veins. She has charmed me with her fierce "warrior" "badass" voice and I am hooked. *"I see you/yes, you poet/you who lives behind the misty veil/dwelling in the border/between this world/and a hundred other/shadow worlds…"* An excerpt from her exquisite 'Poet's Love Song.' And this from 'Loss is an Ocean'- *"how many empty shapes have been etched on my soul like shadow like negatives of photographs from those who have been torn away from this world from my life by the raging tides?"* If you are a poetry lover this book absolutely needs to be on your bookshelf. If you are not poetry lover, you just may become one after reading Ray's *Composition of a Woman*. It is certainly a book that won't be forgotten!"
~Melody Lee, *Season of the Sorceress*

"*Composition of a Woman* is an incredibly crafted volume of poetic nuts and bolts.

Read it slow, savor each piece, and let its strength empower you.

This is a must for every poetic library."
~Alfa, *Silent Squall*

**Books
written by
Christine E. Ray**

The Myths of Girlhood

Composition
of a
Woman
by Christine E. Ray

Composition of a Woman
© 2019 Christine E. Ray

Cover Design by Mitch Green

Editors: Kindra M. Austin
             Georgia Park

All rights reserved.
Printed in the United States of America.

No part of this book may be used, stored in a system retrieval system, or transmitted, in any form or in any means—by electronic, mechanical, photocopying, recording, or reproduced in any manner whatsoever—without written permission from the author, except in the case of brief quotations embodied in critical articles and reviews.

For information, address Indie Blu(e) Publishing.
indieblucollective@gmail.com
Published in the United States of America by Indie Blu(e) Publishing.

ISBN: 978-1-7328000-7-6
Library of Congress Control Number: 2019950886

Dedication

To my Mount Holyoke Alumna sisters who encouraged me to claim my voice, and more importantly, convinced me that I had something valuable to say.

Acknowledgements

Although writing is often a solitary pursuit, the journey of creating a book is not. I owe thanks to many who assisted in the evolution of *Composition of a Woman*.

Kindra M. Austin- Thank you for bravely taking on the first draft of the manuscript and for knowing just what this book should be called. Your love and support throughout the process was invaluable. You are a rock star.

Georgia Park- Thank you for being your glorious, wonderful self and for your unflagging support, enthusiasm, common sense, flexibility, and sense of humor. You went completely above and beyond to help make this book its best self and I am deeply in your debt.

Dennis Earley- Thank you for throwing me a lifeline when I was suffering from one of the most profound depressions of my life. You kept me afloat more days than you know my friend! Thank you for patiently reading draft after draft of this manuscript and offering the tough love when I needed it.

Candice Louisa Daquin- Thank you for the gift of your friendship, your unwavering belief in my writing, astute feedback, and beautiful review of the finished project. It means the world.

Nicole Lyons- Thank you for being a blazing star in the heavens who awes and inspires me daily. It is an honor to have you in my corner and to have you read and review *Composition of a Woman*.

Mitch Green- Thank you for not firing me as a client and patiently working with me until I had a cover that felt just right for my first book. You were a pleasure to work with and your artwork takes my breath away.

Aunt Chookie- You always saw my inner writer and reminded me often throughout the years how important her voice was. I believe you would be pleased to finally see me in print. You are never far from my thoughts.

Kevin, Elijah and Al- Thank you for not believing I was crazy when I suddenly decided at 50 that I wanted to be a writer. I know that my passion for writing and inability to say 'no' to an interesting project has been unexpected- as well as pretty damn disruptive of our family life. Thank you for always giving me the room to be me and for your endless patience with my chaotic creativity, Skypes and IMs at all hours of the day and night with writers in different time zones, and the piles of paper on every flat surface of the house. I love you all to pieces and I couldn't have done this without you.

Contents

Foreword xiii
This Body Is Not an Apology xvii
The Body Politic 3
Vibrational Sensory Loss 4
Seeking Balance 5
My Right Foot 6
Morning, My Nemesis 8
Imposter 9
My Robotic Leg 10
Accordion Folds 12
Sensory Integration 13
EMG 15
Adventures in Neurology 17
Smart Mouth 19
F Words 20
Static 21
Anticlimax 23
Word Play 24
Glass and Thorns 26
Lost Key 28

Encroaching Darkness	33
Melancholia	34
Baby's Black Balloon	35
I Am the Sorrow	37
Empty	38
Origami	40
Misty Blue	42
Safekeeping	44
Please, Baby Please	46
Brilliant Madness	48
Seeing Red	50
The Bell Jar	52
The Shape of Water	57
Memory Brushes Past	58
Marked	60
My Attic Room	61
Wonder	63
Wish for Wings	64
Diving Deep and Surfacing	66
Dragons and Peonies	68
The Taste of Citrus	71
Fire	72
Saturday Afternoon Poetry	73

Drawing Down the Moon	74
Killing Me Softly	75
I Want. .	76
Crystalline Memory	79
Writing on the Wall	80
Kaleidoscope	83
Chasing Sandcastles	84
Chained	86
Operator, I'd Like to Place a Call	87
Messages in the Night Sky	89
Mementos	90
Papa, Please Get the Moon for Me	91
Mother's Day	93
The Ache of My Bones	95
Prayer for the Dead	96
Pinprick of Loss	97
A Suitable Period of Mourning	98
Memorial	100
Song of the Dead	101
I Say That I Lost You	102
Waltz of Spirits	104
Lockets	105
Altered Carbon	107

Loss is an Ocean	108
Where the Sidewalk Ends	113
What Little Girls are Made Of	115
The Bluest Eyes	117
Bad Feminist	119
Sister Outsider	121
I Will Wear Red	123
The Never-ending Story	124
Shrill: Notes from a Loud Woman	126
What We're Told Not to Talk About	127
We Should All Be Feminists	129
Feminists Don't Wear Pink and Other Lies	132
Wonder Woman	134
Black Roses and Moonlight	137
Where the Mountain Meets the Moon	138
I Am the Woman	139
The Sins of My Father	141
That Was Then, This Is Now	143
Lilith	144
Indigo	146
Raven	147
When God Was a Woman	149
We Are the Witches	151

What Makes a Woman	153
Seed	155
Stepping Off the Spiral Path	157
This Bridge Called My Back	159
In Search of Our Mother's Gardens	161
Lost Voice	163
I Want To Fall In Love Again	165
Woman Seeking Poetry	167
I Am	168
Poet's Love Song	170
On Becoming a Poet	173

Foreword

Christine E. Ray's celebrated website, Brave & Reckless, subtitled "Reclaiming my Inner Badass at Age 50," made its debut in October 2016 with the gem "What Every Woman Knows," a response piece to video footage where then Republican Presidential candidate Trump made his infamous "grab them by the pussy" comment. Christine started showcasing her fierce, furious, and often funny poetry on this blog at the tender age of fifty, the same year she got her first tattoo, after working as a clinical social worker and a family interventionalist for twenty years. When I debuted my own politically motivated poetry blog only a month after Brave & Reckless launched, I almost immediately began drawing inspiration and support from Christine. We weren't the only ones coming out of the woodwork to write from a special place of rage during that fall of 2016, but Christine was among the most talented. She has a gift for turning her own trauma into triumph, and perhaps it is due to her career in human services that she is so adept in inspiring others to do the same. Together, we joined Sudden Denouement, and encouraged more writers to emerge.

Since those early days, Christine has become extremely accomplished in the poetry world, creating new platforms for indie writers, winning awards, and creating books. It's fair to say that the only surprising thing about her is her poetry, as I have become accustomed to her consistently clearing the cobwebs out of old ideas and outfitting them with dazzling lights, discovering new writers, and plotting to help Sudden Denouement take over the world.

This is not to say that her legacy overshadows her prolific words. Christine's poetry continuously stands out as the most likely to provoke auditory reactions from her readers. I chuckled, gasped, and moaned during the reading of this manuscript. One of Christine's standout qualities is the ability to add a dash of humor, inspiration, and strength to dire situations, and that quality is alive and well within these pages.

Composition of a Woman is a page-turner, and that's rare for a poetry book. With each poem, the reader is left wondering where Christine will take us next and which form she will use as her mode of transport. The first section of the book, "Nerve", is composed of poems about physical ailments and medical interventions. The subject of bodily dysfunction generally causes me anxiety, and yet I found myself laughing out loud at Christine's playful descriptions. Why can't her right foot behave, when the left foot is tired too but certainly isn't complaining? If someone went to all the trouble of giving her a robotic leg, why can't she jump higher or run faster? If neoplasm is newly formed material, is it still deciding what it wants to be when it grows up; maybe a mellow houseguest or a liberal arts college sorority pledge?

"Nerve" is followed by "Brain," a sequence of poems which dissect the devastating effects of depression and mental malfunctioning at large. Most of the humor and lightness of "Nerve" flutters gently away once we become immersed in "Brain," leaving us surrounded with the shards of a woman. These poems are stunning in their singularity and give the impression of struggling to stay afloat in a deathly calm body of water while a storm rages above. As with all the sections in *Composition of a Woman*, we sense that we are seeing her through a lifetime of these experiences and leaving off where she stands today.

The curtain closes swiftly on "Brain" and the spotlight swivels over to "Breast" and "Rib," which both hold achingly real remnants of romance. "Breast" is sweet, sensual, and nostalgic in its depiction of a relationship, and the loss of that certain love in "Rib" is personal and gut wrenching. These are poems that woo and subsequently destroy. I think a vital function of any poem, especially a love poem, is to at once tell a unique story and make it relatable enough that readers can claim it for their own. Christine has mastered this art. In "Breast," she captures the giddiness and calm wholeness we all feel once we have found a partner. In "Rib," she treats us to wild depictions of neon graffiti and sea salt in soup pots to illustrate her longing and ruminations on the loss of that partner. In "Breast," we also get our first glimpse of Christine's hidden talent, which is prose. Christine's prose pieces are so rich in detail that one can slip into them as luxuriously as a warm, scented bath.

The final section, "Blood," is a well-rounded finale that offers the reader a taste of all Christine has been holding back hitherto. These poems show Christine's place as a woman in a world which is often filled with strife, unrealistic expectations, and burdens that are impossible to carry alone. Her final battle cry seems to be a call for all poets, especially women, to unite. Christine E. Ray could write an entire book on the unification of women alone. The many facets of this divergent poet that are exposed throughout *Composition of a Woman* lead the reader to believe we may look forward to many more poetry books from her. In this last section, she prevails as a charmingly brazen, tough and tender wild thing.

Georgia Park, *Quit Your Day Job and Become a Poet Out of Spite*

This Body Is Not an Apology

this body
cleverly constructed
of blood and bone
muscle and sinew
has not always been
my safe house
others did their best
to paint its innocence
shame red
self-hatred black
carved the words
Lolita
Whore
Bitch
under my skin
rendering this body
an iron maiden
a scold's bridle
a tomb

this body
scaffolded on
an inheritance of madness
and misfiring neurons
has been brought
to the knees
by emotional
and physical pain
this body
ever changing
has not always

been my ally
a friend
at times
an enigma
a stranger
an enemy

this body
keeper of my soul
my essence
weathered my past
survived being
carved hollow by loss
this body
has bled crimson
cried oceans
howled with rage
embraced lovers
birthed babies
rejected expectations
of what a woman should be
could be
has dreamed universes
yet to be discovered
within me

this body
my body
that I continue to broker
peace with
that I have learned to respect
if not always cherish
has protected me

through five decades
vulnerable child
headstrong, obstinate teen
mother
survivor
fierce warrior woman
but this body
my body
will never be an apology

Nerve

Christine E. Ray

The Body Politic

there is an unknown thief
black-clad
masked vigilante
stealing into my nights
robbing me
of things
I once took
for granted
hand
leg
foot
now unpredictable strangers
I struggle to learn
their new language
I must
broker truces
new alliances
keep this country
called *body*
running smoothly
until underlying
political tensions identified
conflicts resolved
or
if necessary
new borders negotiated

Vibrational Sensory Loss

I am routinely pricked with pins
sensations disturbingly
do not match
asymmetry
my right hand
right leg
become phantoms
their volume dialed down
muted
ghosts of former selves
prone to unpredictable behavior
I keep rubbing my right hand
trying to show it
what it is like to *feel*
'remember' I implore
it does not have ears
I am afraid
of disintegration

Seeking Balance

could not walk
toe to heel
balance tipped
lost my footing
and a little of my
nerve
read the messages
in the blood
magnetic
personalities
breathing down
my neck
no longer able to
keep the beat

Composition of a Woman

My Right Foot

on Wednesday night
my right foot went on strike
declaring that unsafe working conditions
too much unpaid overtime
and general lack of appreciation
from the management
made continuing unacceptable
impossible even
as we were walking up a steep hill
at the time
after a very long day
I was not amused
I tried flattery
cajoling
threats
and finally resorted to just dragging
my uncooperative extremity along
muttering under my breath
the whole time
accusing it of being churlish
acting like a petulant child
refusing to be a team player
reminding it that my left foot was tired too
but it certainly wasn't complaining
my right foot
finally started to cooperate again
but sulked the rest of the way home

Christine E. Ray

damn ungrateful foot

Composition of a Woman

Morning, My Nemesis

open one eye
clock tells woeful tale
I overslept
again
sit slowly so room doesn't spin
drunk-stagger to dress
lean my back against wall
to keep balance
looking every inch as bad
as I feel
numbness becomes radiating pain
taking my breath away
seems ironic
shouldn't it hurt less
if I have lost sensation?
try not to drop anything on the floor
I no longer bend
sometimes the past catches me cold
leaves me stuck
in the middle of the room
trapped

Christine E. Ray

Imposter

my right foot and I
are on the outs
again
I keep telling it
what I want it to do
but sometimes it just sits there
unresponsive
It *looks* like my right foot
it *feels* like my right foot
but it's as if it has forgotten
what it means to be *foot*
forgotten what it means
to coordinate with *leg*
my left foot is irritated
by the extra work
my left hand is suspicious
says my right foot must be an imposter
thinks we shouldn't trust it
calls it *faux foot*
my right hand is quiet
wise
under the circumstances
it is weak
losing its grip

Composition of a Woman

My Robotic Leg

someone has replaced
my original right leg
with a robotic leg
must have happened
while I was sleeping
it looks like my old leg
carries out the same basic
functions
bends
flexes
supports my weight
(most of the time)
and yet it feels
other
uneven sensitivity to stimuli
rubbery in places
I am increasingly convinced
that I could
stick a hunting knife
in my mid-thigh
and feel nothing
until the synthetic blood
running down my leg
reached my calf
my ankle
it is glitchy
prone to

Christine E. Ray

acts of rebellion
I have never seen
the wires and microchips
cogs and gears
but I imagine they
are in there someplace
I contemplate
an excavation
you would think that
if someone went to all
the trouble of giving me
a robotic leg
it would be able to run faster
jump higher
penetrate cement walls
with a single kick
but my new leg
shows no sign of any
special capabilities
you'd think
I'd at least
be able to read my email
on my knee
open a beer
with my bionic toes

Accordion Folds

there is a point
where the pain starts
radiates out
in a geometric
arc
compresses
folds
reconfigures me
like an open fan
of a courtesan
I am a
dense network
of twisted muscle
screaming nerves
aching numbness
at pain's core
while my edges
are left thin
fragile
transparent

Sensory Integration

when my brain goes haywire
I think I must have developed
late-onset sensory integration disorder
the sun burns my eyes
the birds chirp their Spring songs
much too loudly for me
beloved coffee overwhelms me
with its roasted aroma
I admire the way that liberated
warm weather dresses swing down Locust Walk
rayon, silk, satin, linen drape beautifully
make their wearers walk with confidence
I like the feel of these fabrics
against my fingertips
but am only able to tolerate
utilitarian cotton knits
against my back
my stomach
thighs
my skin
now a single exposed nerve
perceives anything else
as sandpaper
rubbing me raw
the acupuncturist palpates
my numb right leg
looking for the best place

Composition of a Woman

to insert the hair thin needle
in hopes of returning sensation
to my errant limb
her fingertip finds a meridian point
so excruciatingly painful
on the inside of my knee
I practically levitate
off the table
she smiles broadly
as she announces, "We have a winner!"
indeed

Christine E. Ray

EMG

The overhead light has a gridded metal cover
that reminds me of the old-fashioned ice cube trays
my grandmother had
with levers that released the frozen squares
with a satisfying crack
I feel oddly vulnerable waiting alone
wearing nothing but my panties and bra
under today's utilitarian hospital gown
with its overly complicated ties
that took me too long to decode
in a way that I didn't earlier this week
when my breasts were compressed
between inflexible plastic plates
while the fancy 3D camera rotated
in a state-of-the-art 180 degree arc around my body
there is a natural comradery
between women of a certain age
dutifully reporting for their yearly mammogram
that I miss while I wait for my neurologist
and her technician to take turns
shooting electricity through my misbehaving limbs
the word *electromyography*
rolling on my tongue
I stare at the ceiling as the minutes tick by
ruminate about the other patients
who held introspected vigil in the waiting room
while I waited for my name to be called discreetly

Composition of a Woman

in accordance with HIPPA
wondering if not so long ago
before their canes
their walkers
their motorized wheelchairs
they were like me

Christine E. Ray

Adventures in Neurology

the phlebotomist who likes my tatts
and is disappointed that Villanova
is out of the playoffs
admits to me that this is the
first vitamin e level he has ever
drawn in his career
I am much more intrigued
with the copper level
he tells me that usually he
only sees orders for copper
when someone had had a hip
replacement and there is concern
about metal leakage
good to know
new body parts will
be examined by magnetic waves
later this week
in effort to solve my mysteries
I will think about voxels
and Lululemon yoga pants
to distract myself
in the clanging narrow tube
my body's betrayal
does not sit easily with me
I value my independence
was not prepared for
shaving my legs to become

Composition of a Woman

a high risk activity at 51
I still hope
that a change in pharma
or a nutritional supplement
may result in a return to equilibrium
but it seems prudent to
contemplate my options
should my limbs continue to
go rogue
there is always waxing
and pedicures
Dragon software
my left hand could learn new tricks
pick up some slack
my coworkers and I agree
that I am *way* too badass
for an old lady cane
if this is my new neurological destiny
I need something steampunk
or at least with a skull on the handle
this is *me* we're talking about

Christine E. Ray

Smart Mouth

the profanity I utter
rising from sitting
to standing
is sharp
salty
as hip
and knee
joints crack open
like lobster claws
and muscle fibers
tear with a rip
we do not wash
mouths out with soap
in this house
words of power
are allowed

F Words

fatigue hangs on me
like heavy ornaments
on a late February
Christmas tree
branches brittle and bare
needles dropping to floor
carpeted
in half-finished projects
incomplete thoughts
good–but soon forgotten– intentions
so much aromatic debris
carelessly spilling around my feet

Christine E. Ray

Static

the low buzz of pain
over my eyebrows
has moved from white noise
that I can block out
with conscious effort
to the weight
of a small hippo
pushing down
into the front
of my skull
leaving the back
of my neck
throbbing
my left eyelid droopy
my thoughts
in tatters
I reach ineffectively
for ideas as they float by
try to concentrate
on everything
I had hoped
to do today
but the inside of my head
is filled with stinging wasps
and resembles the screen
of my grandmother's
13 inch black and white TV

Composition of a Woman

at 2 am
I am nothing
but the snow
of static
again

Anticlimax

weighed down
by sterile syllables
that do not roll off
tongue with ease
taste of examination rooms
rubbing alcohol
hand sanitizer
poked and prodded under glare of fluorescent lights
that make the blossoming head pain
triggered by waiting room perfume
aftershave
turn into steady throb over right eye
not enough time to sound out
new labels
cypher meaning and implications
before polite dismissal
with a handshake
instructions to come back in four months
before being replaced
by the next number
in the queue
pages covered in medical hieroglyphics
clutched in hand
while walking toward exit sign
'now what?'
echoing in tired ears

Word Play

neoplasm of uncertain behavior
neo + plasm
= newly formed material
which apparently is still deciding
what it wants to be when it grows up
could be a mellow houseguest
could become an invading conqueror
neoplasm of uncertain behavior
is biding its time
contemplating life choices
maybe a small liberal arts college
or maybe a large university
pledge a sorority?
play lacrosse?
try out for an a capella group?
maybe it wants to go pre-med
or study creative writing
neoplasm of uncertain behavior
seems to find the climate hospitable
is laying down roots
like the periwinkle in the yard
that is crowding out the ivy
but no delicate purple blooms
neoplasm of uncertain behavior
'uncertain'
makes it sound almost edgy
badass

Christine E. Ray

new name for a punk band?
incidental findings
could be the band's first hit single

Glass and Thorns

Betrayal is an inside job
wrecked by muscle and
joints
neurons and
neurotransmitters
mitochondrial mutiny
lays waste
to formerly silver tongue
now struggling to find words
that used to flow like
ink through fountain pen
fatigue hangs round neck
chain woven of boulders, glass shards &
thorns
muscle spasms contort me
into balloon animal shapes
so alien, so grotesque
that they frighten the village children
like the pick axe
I plant above right eye
in hopes of blessed relief
don't mind the blood
it's barely an inconvenience
during insomniac ruminations
about long dormant-mutations
coded in DNA turned
time bombs

Christine E. Ray

that ripped through my life
casualty count still being assessed
by medics in white coats
who write cryptic words
on shiny clipboards
while I bleed

Composition of a Woman

Lost Key

the transformation
was so slow
so gradual
that I was unaware
bones had turned glass
joints brass clockwork
until they seized
from lack of lubrication
made me stumble gracelessly
onto cracked tiles
hands once strong
supple
now tremble
fail to grasp
fail to open
jars and tubs
of balms
of potions
that clutter dresser top
displacing brushes
jewelry with delicate clasps
making empty promises
to ease aches
pains
I now wind down
an underpowered automaton
dust a fine coating on pale skin

Christine E. Ray

words once nimble on my tongue
swim in and out of view
bright as koi
frustratingly elusive
in brain rendered too sluggish
too viscous
to gather them
in silver butterfly nets
and set them free

Brain

Christine E. Ray

Encroaching Darkness

darkness is washing over me
like spilled black ink
viscous puddles on my skin
like oxygen-rich blood
iron-tinged air
darkness is icy breath
on the back of my neck
skeletal fingers
sensually stroking my spine
leaving me no-comfort cold
painful goosebumps
raised on my pale skin
darkness is wrapping its gray smoky tendrils
around my throat
caressing me like a lover
who does not respect
my safe word
tightening ever so slowly
into a noose
stealing my breath
stealing my voice
seeking to obliterate
to lay waste

Melancholia

steeped dark
in the solitude of my thoughts
I lay forgotten
in an empty room
as if poured from a pitcher
onto smooth glass
thin
transparent
idly reach out index finger
to trace deepening shadows
on the white wall
traveling contours
of an imaginary landscape
that I long to escape to
as twilight falls soft
silent
around me

Christine E. Ray

Baby's Black Balloon

I long to be buoyant
an updraft
to lift your wings
allow you to
glide thermals
gracefully
your eyes closed
in exhilaration
as crisp air
fills your lungs
but today
I am a
black balloon
thrust upon you
unexpectedly
tied to your wrist
with dirty
frayed string
that chafes
at your skin
a cold iron shackle
I do not mean to
weigh you down
with a force of gravity
previously found
only on Jupiter
I hover inches

Composition of a Woman

above the ground
heavy
deflated
waiting for
my final descent

I Am the Sorrow

some days I do not just feel sorrow
some days I *am* the sorrow
I am the grey sky
that threatens spitting snow
I am the heaviness in your limbs
your shuffling gait
reluctant to get
where you are expected
 some days
I am the sorrow
the stark, leafless, skeletal
branches of the trees
dwelling in the in-between
of not-quite late autumn
not-quite early winter
that borderline of the seasons
when light is dwindling
and darkness grows
some days
I am the wistfulness
that deep longing for your younger self
when time stretched endlessly
before you
the world full of possibility
and the crisp taste of golden fruit

Empty

words and
phrases
lay abandoned
on every flat surface
and on the floor
below me
so much glittering
confetti that
crunches under
my bare feet
the party over
guests long gone
home
leaving me alone
adrift
among empty wine glasses
plates of half-eaten promise
I feel simultaneously sick
from fare
far too rich
with false hope
while burning
with my hunger
to communicate
to connect
I am hollowed out
stomach as empty

Christine E. Ray

as my soul
tired to the bone
but unable to face
the long crawl to
my bed
I settle into
an empty corner
lean my head back
into the shadow
and fade away. . .

Origami

I cannot
be broken
twice
but life is
doing its
damn best
to bend me
fold me
into painful
sharp
origami shapes
crane
butterfly
swan
turtle
frog
dragon
over and over
deep creases form
in my skin
my muscles twist
bones scream
heart aches from compression
soul cries mercy
as I contort
become unrecognizable
fall to the ground

Christine E. Ray

like crumpled paper

Misty Blue

angel from my left shoulder
is on vacation
reading *Kafka at the Shore*
in a ruffled white tankini
while sipping Shirley Temples
sends quaint postcards
scrawled in pink ink
"*Weather is beautiful, glad you aren't here*"
her A's all hearts of course
devil on my right shoulder
is all business
rocks Prada
Manola Blahniks
has no interest in inciting a pussy riot
or taking me out to a rave
taking me down a peg
brings her joy
like most mean girls
her voice could etch glass
painted on smile never wavers
while she drips venom drop by drop
down my naked ear
fraud
she hisses
fake
wannabe
you suck

Christine E. Ray

loooooooooser
perhaps I could drown her out
with sprightly show tunes
but the radio station is stuck
on Etta James
all that will play
is the blues

Safekeeping

darkness has descended again
the fall a white-gripped
drop on a roller coaster
my unraveling
my disintegration
rapid
terrifying
there is little comfort
other than that found
wrapped in strong arms
bare skin to bare skin
relaxed breath synchronized
kinetic thoughts stilled
to manageable speed
rest of the world
held at bay
for precious moments
as I fragment
lose structural integrity
devolve into primordial ooze
I wonder if others I have
given pieces of myself to
remember who I once was
can hand back strands
of mitochondrial DNA
my starved cells can engulf
can replicate

Christine E. Ray

building blocks
for wholeness
entrusted to the safekeeping
of others

Please, Baby Please

I have never written
about the nights
I lay awake
watching time crawl
across the shadowed ceiling
wondering what I might find
with morning's light
I have never written
about the horrific images
my anxiety creates
vivid film shorts that play
one after another
on an endless loop
I have never written
about what it is like
to lay there helpless
not knowing
if the emptiness
and despair
that nip at your heels
like a pitbull
have finally become the undertow
that pulls you beyond my reach
I considered sleeping
on your bedroom floor
holding vigil
throwing my very body

between you
and the abyss
but you can barely tolerate
me knowing about the pills
you hoarded and swallowed
this further invasion
of your space
your privacy
your agency
will only further fray our edges
and right now
you need me
however inadequate
I may seem
time has gifted me
two important truths:
this devil depression
will not always torment you
with such bruising intensity
please, baby please
just hang on a little bit longer
I have also learned
control is an illusion
I cling to
and that all my love
all my vigilance
all my sleepless nights
will have no influence
over what you
choose to do

Brilliant Madness

I live in a state
of brilliant madness
teetering on the apex
of a craggy mountain
balanced atop a skateboard
precarious
least shift of weight
momentary loss of focus
could result in long careen
into a ravine
of sharp rocks
fallen branches
brackish water
it is exhausting
and exhilarating
my thoughts
tumbling
exploding
atoms in a cyclotron
thick blue dots
moving in clear viscous liquid
of tall glass cylinder
reaching for the ceiling
reaching for sky
at times they synchronize
military formation
at others they collide

in complete anarchy
I have been waking
in one of two states
words pulling at me
rousing me
demanding
that I sit in front of the
impersonal screen
serve as a conduit
as they take shape
write themselves
the other state
suspended animation
frozen in time
trapped in silence
unable to muster
a single word
a single truth
terrifying
I admit to myself
if to no one else
deep ambivalence toward
jagged little pharma
sitting on the kitchen table
that may save my life
but steal
this brilliant madness

Seeing Red

blue and white capsules
ingested daily
devour my melancholy baby
always ravenous
unsatisfied
they strip protective coating
off vulnerable neurons
leaving them raw
excitable
the faintest whisper
or intimation
that I fail to please
am not enough
makes irritation rise a
red tide
up my spinal column
forcing fluid rage
into hollows
ossification has crudely
carved into each
vertebrae
stiff-backed
bristling
lupine claws extend
gruff growl grows
low in my throat
and I am prepared

Christine E. Ray

in that heartbeat
to shred tender flesh-
yours *or* mine-
clean to the bone

The Bell Jar

the heart
of my madness
beats wildly
beneath polished glass
its feathered limbs
twisting
turning
frantically
a living thing
fighting desperately
to be free
it is both monstrous
and
achingly beautiful
as it contorts
onyx and plum
catching the light
before it shifts
midnight and crimson
it is pitiable
as it throws itself
again and again
against curved walls
I struggle
with deep longing
to release it
cradle it in my arms

Christine E. Ray

croon a lullaby
but like all feral things
sooner or later
it will turn on me
bite me viciously
on my breast
until I bleed
impale me with
razor-sharp talons
and not release me
until long after
it has taken flight

Christine E. Ray

Breast

Christine E. Ray

The Shape of Water

we do not need words
we do not need a shared
written language
we have eyes that truly see
lips that speak a common tongue
a shared palate for the aroma
the taste
of the salt that glitters
on each other's skin
when we flow like silk
against each other
and boundaries dissolve
like sea foam
at dawn

Memory Brushes Past

memory's delicate tendrils
reach out
brush the nape
of my neck
cause an electric shiver
that courses
down my spine
the past
whispers
syllables
sweet and breathy
that tickle
my ear
remember
it implores
remember
crisp white sheets
whiff of cedar
sound of the ocean
butterfly brush
of eyelashes
against
salty skin
kisses
so soft
they dissolved like sugar
and lemon

Christine E. Ray

on my eager tongue

Marked

we were more than fingerprints
brushed across each other's wrists
we loved recklessly
deeply
dipped our hands
into our souls
pulled out everything we were
before leaving our marks across each other's bodies
I had never seen you more beautiful
than you were
with my handprint
caressing your cheekbone
shimmering across your heart

Christine E. Ray

My Attic Room

You in my attic bedroom in Somerville. Green and tan striped wallpaper inexpertly hung on the deeply slanted walls. Futon on the floor, the smell of warm cedar, window fan lazily stirring the air. Dust particles floating suspended in golden light that falls across the hardwood floor in a diagonal. Your eyes the bluest I have ever seen. Skin so pale it is almost translucent. Your short hair black and curly, surprisingly silky to my touch. Your mint fresh breath against my mouth as if you could breathe for both of us. We try to stay away from each other but we are the drug the other is always craving, we are the hum in each other's blood. You don't tell me how you explain your absence from home and I don't ask. You are the only thing that makes me feel alive. Your soft breasts visible under the ribbed white men's undershirt that sticks to your skin with summer sweat. You twist your fingers in the belt loops of my shorts, pulling my hips closer to yours. Our mouths always hungry, our bodies straining to meld into each other through layers of thin cotton. We are liquid fire in each other's arms. The feel of my hands tangled in your hair, the hitch in your breath when I trace your throat with my lips. We tell ourselves that it is just kissing, that as long as our shirts and shorts are on this is not an affair. We rationalize this wildfire passion to ourselves, to each other, even when we arch our bodies into each other, even when you give me your gentle and your

Composition of a Woman

fierce, even when you call in the middle of the night to say that you cannot stop thinking about me, that you can't live without my apricot kiss.

Wonder

you are a gift
waiting to be opened
wrapped in brown paper
string
I am not fooled
by such humble wrappings
yet still I catch my breath
when the string releases
and you unwind your heart
into my cupped hands
I am filled with awe
with wonder
at the treasure
that lies within

Wish for Wings

you stand with your back to me
vulnerable
silent
I, transfixed
by how your wings attach
to blades of shoulders
already burdened by the weight
of humanity's sorrow
of the demands
of gods with no mercy
how can mere bone
bear this additional weight
of a thousand ivory feathers
without folding
to the ground?
the strip of bare skin
that separates
your magnificent wings
calls to me
my hand reaches out
palm extended
to trace
the path of smooth muscle
the intake of your breath
the rapid beats of our hearts
the only sound
as I press my cheek

Christine E. Ray

to that vulnerable spot
you are stiff for a moment
before relaxing fully
against me
guiding my arms firmly
around your waist
holding them tight
accepting the comfort
of my warm
human touch

Diving Deep and Surfacing

you are swift moving water
traveling through dense forest
twisting
turning
through midnight landscape
fireflies and Luna moths
crisscross
your body
in a dazzling display
of bioluminescence
while wood nymphs
waltz on your mossy banks
to the chorus of crickets
and the hoots of snow white owls
I am the waxing moon
hanging in the indigo night
cool and remote
my silver light
glittering upon your surface
where I see myself reflected
I am almost beautiful
as you flow over rocks and logs
up hills and down vales
then rush over cliffs
you become a waterfall
and sing me a siren song
of longing

Christine E. Ray

of heart's desire
until recklessly into your depths
I plunge

Dragons and Peonies

the skin I am in
longs to become acquainted
with the skin you are in
our eyes meet
across the room
and I forget that
we are not alone
we came tonight with
a larger group of friends
but we are increasingly
attuned to each other
there is something in the air
tonight
I like the
boldness of your gaze
as you keep catching my eye
your snaggle tooth grin
the sound of your laughter
at some inside joke
the tantalizing glimpse
of ink peeking out of
your shirt sleeve
I wonder what it will look like
lined up against the ink
on my arm
my gentle peonies
against your fiery dragon

Christine E. Ray

your jeans and ironic tee
hint of lanky muscles
of steel
that I think will fit nicely
against my curves
I cannot stop the smile
and slight blush from
crossing my face
you seem to be
reading my mind
across the room
your cocked eyebrow
and slow lazy smile
indicate to me
that you are as
distracted by me
as I am by you
I watch you make your
excuses
to your friends
that you have been
only half paying attention to
before you saunter
my way
when you are finally
standing in front of me
I feel the warmth coming
off your body
catch a whiff of your clean scent
there is a sparkle in your eye

Composition of a Woman

'*shall we?*' is all you need to say
it feels as natural as breathing
when you reach for my hand
and we leave this crowd behind
aware only of each other

Christine E. Ray

The Taste of Citrus

silken black blindfold
covers eyes
feel your thumb
tracing my bottom lip
'open up' you say
I hesitate only briefly
before i obey
tongue and teeth greeted
with sweet-tart taste of ripe
blood orange
juices running
down chin
collarbone
bare breasts
you feed me more segments unhurriedly
citrus dripping
skin sticky
your lips
long and lingering on mine
before trailing down to drink
sweet-tart juice
from my warm skin

Composition of a Woman

Fire

The sheets with tiny pink rosebuds, incongruously innocent, are tangled beneath us. Your lips travel slowly down from my earlobe to my neck, marking your territory. You stop at my collarbone; nipping it gently with your teeth before lifting your head to look at me.

Our shirts are lost somewhere on the floor, my bra discarded on the bed along with our socks. Jeans and underwear create the only barrier that separates us from each other's skin. I want to know your skin as well as I know my own. Every scar, every freckle, every tattoo, every perfect imperfection.

Your hair is damp with sweat as you balance above me. Your eyes are dark, intense, questioning. I involuntarily bite my lip. I am already anticipating your fingers deftly unbuttoning, unzipping, removing the obstacles. You take me out of my always busy head, reminding me that I am flesh, I am fire when I am with you.

Christine E. Ray

Saturday Afternoon Poetry

bare skin glides against my rough edges
like warm sand you buff my contours smooth
mouth tracing the trail of my vertebrae
you become cartographer of my ridges and valleys
before breathing electricity along my spine
bold fingertips find the places I ache
work me like clay
patiently loosen the knots
I have tied myself into
until I exhale the pain
the tension
into your kiss
your palms
become silk flowing through your arms
sighs against your neck
arching into your body's poetry
until we are a tangle of arms and legs
against damp sheets
minds floating free
no longer bound by time and frail flesh

Drawing Down the Moon

bare alabaster arms raised to the heavens
I sing the ancient songs to the endless night
I draw down the moon from the velvet
cradle her in my arms like a babe
bathe in her icy luminescence
draw it deep into my body
until my skin is translucent
cool to the touch
I am filled with the light
of a thousand stars
and the wolves howl
to the empty sky

you contain the fire of the sun
golden and crimson
it slips through your veins
ripples beneath your skin
dances in your eyes
amber that holds my image fixed
we are holy, consecrated
equals worthy of each other
performing an ancient rite
that cleanses the earth
and ignites the night

Killing Me Softly

haunting poetry sung
to languid strum of acoustic guitar
penetrated my ear
untied my heartstrings
left me bleeding
longing
on hardwood floor

I Want. . .

I want. . .
I whisper
to empty rooms
air so chilly
that words float
ghostly moths
frozen in the mist of my breath
unprepared for them to linger there
echo with meaning
give voice to hungers
I tell myself
I do not have
full of guilt
fascination
I trace the letters
with silver pink fingertips
caress the curves and lines
say it louder
bolder
I want. . .
I want. . .

Rib

Crystalline Memory

we fell into memory
like sea salt
into soup pot
crystalline structure
losing integrity
dissolving
into warm liquid
like the bath water
you poured me
scented with lavender
when we belonged to each other
we would lie close
skin to skin on long winter nights
under thick blankets
our boundaries dissolving
like foam on our tongues

Writing on the Wall

I read the
writing on the wall
neon graffiti
composed of
cryptic symbols
stunning words
of power
rage
grief
that sting
my bare skin like sleet
ice crystals that burn
and freeze on contact
I recognize your
artist's tag
I long to
pull out
cans of spray paint
from my battered
backpack
connect the dots
with hunter green
soften the edges
silver and mauve
rewrite the narrative
midnight blue
but this is not

Christine E. Ray

my territory
I am unsure of
my welcome
on your turf
these days
I reluctantly
turn away
and walk
city streets
concrete and steel
broken glass
strewn sidewalks
to my 3rd floor
walk-up
rows of deadlocks
and chains
on the door
never certain if
their purpose is to
keep others out
or keep my creative
madness contained
in this room
of my own
blank canvases
await
I pause
briefly
consider
what I want

Composition of a Woman

what I *need*
to express
and lose myself
to the process
weaving words
of love
of healing
spinning dreams
painting longing
etched with light
a thing of
beauty
that you may
never see

Kaleidoscope

we came together
broke apart
glass fragments tossed
in a kaleidoscope
tumbling into each other
beautiful
trembling
symmetrical patterns
captured briefly in the mirror
before the spin of the wheel
pulled us apart
leaving our jewel tone edges
aching from separation

Chasing Sandcastles

you feel
impossibly distant
elusive
the receding tide
I am left chasing sandcastles
before they are reclaimed
by rushing waters
our connection
has become reduced to
collisions in the dark
that throw us off balance
knees and
hearts left aching
I have been
studying the language
of oceans
gazing out
at the horizon
until the
sea blurs
before my eyes
I try to read
the omens
throw the bones
in the crashing waves
play of light
rippling on the water

Christine E. Ray

the surf whispers
over and over
to me that
you are gone
the current has
carried you
far beyond my reach

Chained

silken strands
and finely spun
steel
compose the
knotted memory
that holds you
fast and taut
close to
my heart
despite
gentle tugs
and pulls
they stubbornly
refuse to
relax their grip
each moment
we shared
a hand-tied pearl
in a necklace
of silver thorns
and longing

Christine E. Ray

Operator, I'd Like to Place a Call

the missing of you
feels like a small animal
gnawing at my heart
my world isn't quite right
when I can't be sure
that you are still in it
you have severed yourself
from all modern technology
that you declare
'sources of connected
disconnection'
it leaves me with hands empty of you
I think about placing a call
the old-fashioned way
but I am all out of quarters
and payphones have become almost extinct
only found in the Smithsonian
next to the manual typewriter
you wouldn't open the door
to a stranger
I know you would appreciate the whimsy
of a tin can stretched between our houses
but I don't have 2,700 miles of string
I try to connect with you through the ether
grab the thread of your vibrating frequency
but your beautiful colors
are not calling out to me

Composition of a Woman

the way they usually do
I must resort to inscribing a message
into the night sky
letting you know that you are loved
that you are missed

Christine E. Ray

Messages in the Night Sky

I look to the stars
in this onyx night
trace constellations
with tentative fingertip
my heart aching to find
the shape of you
in raised dots
that read like braille
to my soul

Mementos

I keep you in a basket
at the foot of my bed
that I can grab quickly
in case of fire
or other emergency
you are tucked in among
postcards from exotic places
fading photographs
handwritten letters
greeting cards signed with love
and other mementos
of my past
that I can't bear to lose

Christine E. Ray

Papa, Please Get the Moon for Me

so many nights
did I gaze
at the stars
wondering
if you stood
on a distant shore
looking up
wistfully
thinking of me
pondering
whether our skies
were the same
I could *almost* imagine
us side by side
your sure hand
pointing out constellations
patiently for me
Orion
Cassiopeia
Ursa Major
Papa-
if you had been there
on that windswept
Cape Cod beach
would you have ruffled
my hair
smiled with pride

Composition of a Woman

affection
and promised me
the moon?

Christine E. Ray

Mother's Day

bittersweet
symphonies
echo
for this
motherless child
it has been
almost two decades
but fingers still itch
to pick up
old-fashioned receiver
on Sundays
punch in your number
tell you about the 90's
Elijah earned on spring finals
hear you laugh that Al
is indeed my karma
roll your eyes
across the miles
at my latest tattoo
we were puzzles
to each other
mismatched pieces
that often
rubbed and chafed
I was never
soft cardboard
was I?

Composition of a Woman

lasered steel perhaps
sharp around the edges
your mysteries
still reveal themselves
from time to time
causing the kaleidoscope
picture I carry
to abruptly spin
rearranging the
colored shards
of myth
and memory
as your fractalled image
shifts into something
new
an unfinished narrative
for me to ponder

Christine E. Ray

The Ache of My Bones

I feel you in my bones
deep within the marrow
your name written
crimson and ivory
on platelets
and leukocytes
I reach out my hand
but still you slip away
so much crystalized
phosphorus
crushed calcium
leaving me brittle
hollow
bitter scars of ossification
only proof that you once
dwelled within me

Prayer for the Dead

my heart
dresses in
black lace
when I slide beads slowly
through my practiced hands
their surfaces warm
worn smooth
against calloused
fingertips
it is the tender tissue
of my throat
that stings
as I murmur
their names
one by one
in order of loss
head bowed low
in the candlelight
no omissions are allowed
or I must return
to the beginning
start again
the ritual must be
performed perfectly
at the altar
of my dead

Christine E. Ray

Pinprick of Loss

the loss of you
punctured the night sky
like tiny pinpricks on a black canvas
covering the moon from view
allowing only the smallest rays
of cool silver light
to feather touch
my pale lips
my empty hands

A Suitable Period of Mourning

I do not have a closet
full of mourning clothes
I have never
inked the names of my dead
on my tender forearms
in solemn homage
the list too long
my arms too short
to box with God
I am a motherless child
who grieved too long
for the comfort of others
left me wondering if grief
is considered contagious
a virus?
what is the suitable period of mourning
for loss of my identity
as daughter?
as granddaughter?
we do not mention pregnancy losses
as if they don't count
don't matter
as though the hopes
the dreams
we embraced
for those little balls of cells
were weightless

Christine E. Ray

mere dandelion fluff
in the breeze
we are left
standing alone
in contemplation
of our empty arms
is a man who never held his breathing child
still a father?
a widowed woman still a wife?
a boy who has lost his twin still a brother?
who are we when those we love are lost
and all that remains are their empty shapes on our soul
like Peter Pan's shadow?

Memorial

I find my native tongue
inadequate to speak
the true language of loss
where parts of identity break
from our continent
drifting off in crimson tides.

Christine E. Ray

Song of the Dead

I have learned to carry
my ghosts
with reverence
slip them gently
into my pockets
cradle them close
to carotid pulse
the most loyal
of my companions
lulled by steady beat
of my survivor's heart
borrowed touches through
my fingertips
stolen glances
through my eyes
I am filled with
whispered secrets of
the dead
haunting and
haunted still

Composition of a Woman

I Say That I Lost You

I say that I lost you
as though you were an umbrella
that I carelessly left on the bus
after the summer rain had stopped

I say that I lost you
as though you were a conversation
that I dropped the thread of
when I became
distracted by fireflies dancing outside my window

I say that I lost you
as though you were a book
I insisted that a friend borrow and read
that was never returned

I say that I lost you
as though you were a bet
a wager
I could easily afford to place

to say that I lost you
is to say that the world that I knew has ended
that the universe has been torn violently in two
that time has stopped like a broken pocket watch
whose hands now stand empty
reaching for a tomorrow

Christine E. Ray

that will never come

Waltz of Spirits

the floor stretches before me
black and white checkerboard tile
feet glide soundlessly
to the waltz in my head
my arms arched as if partnered
but empty
silent
transparent forms
swirl around me
lost in the dance
do they know I wonder
that they are behind the veil?
perhaps it only matters
to me
left behind

Christine E. Ray

Lockets

I wear my losses
on a chain
'round my neck
copper
silver
gold
charms
containing locks
of stranded memory
tied with red ribbon
sometimes they are
featherweight
sometimes they weigh
the world
sharp edges prick
at my tender skin

I have carved regret
deep in the palms
of my hands
heather
oak
bittersweet
smoky
from the hearth
where I kneel prostrate
praying to silent gods
for second chances

Composition of a Woman

I am not sure
that I have earned
rough stone floors
abrading chilled knees
punishing me
for my sins

Altered Carbon

I pinned my phosphorus heart
to the crisp linen sleeve
of my mourning suit
where all could see
your initials
carved deep
no matter which face
I choose from the
jars kept at the door
the hold of your memory
remains elemental

Loss is an Ocean

I stand on the shore
of an ocean named Loss
where my eyes are always
drawn to the horizon
scanning encroaching fog
for the outlines
of those I have loved
of those I have lost

how many empty shapes
have been etched on my soul
like shadow
like negatives of photographs
from those who have been torn away
from this world
from my life
by the raging tides?

eulogies
written in my blood
on the golden sands
in calligraphy
words
memories
caging my heart
like delicate silver filigree

Christine E. Ray

I am called to the sea
to sing their names
one by one
to the dawn tide
ancient shanties
of the women who have waited
women who know loss
like an element
a mineral
mixed in the marrow of their bones
I will sing steady and pure
refresh their memories
recall their meaning
for the rising sun
the fading moon
letting nothing be forgotten

Christine E. Ray

Blood

Christine E. Ray

Where the Sidewalk Ends

where did your colt legs carry you
the day you ran away
small pack
set upon
determined shoulders
overstuffed with much-loved books
slightly crushed snacks
a hastily chosen teddy bear?
did you hesitate
before stepping off
the gray pavement
where dandelions
fought their way
through the cracks
raising their yellow
and green heads
with proud resilience?
did you stand
gathering courage
at the edge
where the safe
met the forbidden,
where the sidewalk ends?
did freedom and
danger
dance like twin butterflies
in your stomach

Composition of a Woman

as you took that step
into the unknown?
did you twirl in the late
afternoon sun
thrilled with your daring?
how long did you roam
those green fields
imagining castles on the hill
fairies watching from the trees
a dragon dozing in the cave
before your growling stomach
and the growing dark
lured you back home?

Christine E. Ray

What Little Girls are Made Of

she had always been puzzled
by the idea that little girls
were made of sugar
and spice
and everything nice
in her experience
that's not what
little girls
were made of at all

the mean girls smelled
like cruelty mixed with uncertainty
disdain peppered with insecurity
ravenous hunger and envy

some girls smelled like
saccharine sweetness
and copper wire
wound too tight
always trying to please
to be liked
to be popular

others just wanted
to fly under the radar
to escape the notice
of mean girls who torment

Composition of a Woman

of chameleon girls who offered
friendship only to shun them
the moment the mean girls
or a boy
beckoned

she was a different
kind of girl
the quiet, watchful kind
she had ageless wisdom
in her heart
steel in her spine
fire in her blood
and patience
her time would come

there weren't many
girls like her
but when they brushed
past each other
in school hallways
or crowded streets
the recognition
was like lightning
eyes would meet boldly
and they would smile
the secret smiles
of their kind

Christine E. Ray

The Bluest Eyes

ivory hued dolls
with wavy golden locks
lovingly combed
and styled
sat carefully along
the bedroom shelf
their piercing blue eyes
painted open
in horror
their mouths forming
silent O's
of unheard screams
no protection
no comfort
can they offer
these porcelain witnesses
of the injustices
inflicted upon
her young brown body
by a racist society
by boys
and men
she knew
she trusted
her world
her skin
her psyche
shattered

Composition of a Woman

by such
callous
disregard
unable to bear
their unblinking knowing
any longer
she turns each doll
so they face
the wall
and begins to slowly
painstakingly
sew herself
back together

Christine E. Ray

Bad Feminist

when I only kissed girls
I was accused of being a *man-hater*
when I could braid the hair under my arms
broke disposable razors on my legs
I was called *earthy-crunchy*
when I decided to major in women studies
I became a *bra burner*
when I interrupted men
demanded my turn
I was a *bitch*
when I cared about gay men
contracting HIV
and dying of aids
I was told I had been *co-opted*
when I didn't laugh at
sexist/homophobic/racist/anti-Semitic jokes
they called me a *killjoy*
when I insisted on being inter-sectional
I was labeled a *radical*
when I fell in love with a man
I was marked a *traitor*
when I married him and had children
I was a *sellout*
when I insisted that we did not live
in a post-feminist world
I was called a *dinosaur*
when I started to speak truth about

Composition of a Woman

rape, sexual abuse, and harassment
I was told I was playing *the victim card*
when I turned 50
I was considered *obsolete*
I am not made
for standing on pedestals
you will not find me
cast in bronze as
an exemplar of feminist
wisdom and ideology
I will be in the wings
tripping over my soapboxes
dented megaphone
in my hand

Christine E. Ray

Sister Outsider

Sister Outsider
how many times
have my hazel eyes
bought me the
luxury of blindness?
how many times
has the skin I walk in
this ivory cocoon
insulated me
from your reality?
how many times
have I naively
claimed that we
are all the same
underneath our pigment
as if my bones
had carried
the weight of your
ancestors' chains
as if my blood
knew the acid burn
of your rage
pumping through
your body
as you have been
undermined
underestimated

Composition of a Woman

exploited
pushed aside
excluded from a seat
at the table?
how many times have
I made it *your* job
not mine
to teach me the truth
about your life?
how many times
have I been silent
when I should speak?
how many times
did I patronizingly
assume that I knew what *you* wanted
what you needed
without listening to your voice?
Sister Outsider
how many times
have I failed you?
how many times
will I fall short
and fail you still?

I Will Wear Red

I will wear red
for my sisters whose health is at risk
for my sisters who have been raped
for my sisters who have been battered
for my sisters who are already struggling
to feed hungry children
for my sisters who need to finish
middle school
high school
college
grad school
for my sisters who are just not prepared
I will wear crimson
for their lifeblood
that will spill in back alleys
that will stain
wire hangers
knitting needles
other unsterilized implements
that become their only choice
in a country that questions
their ability
their very right
to choose

The Never-ending Story

a woman speaks
into the void
tries to impart
necessary truth
that actions proposed
will harm the vulnerable
increase suffering
for those
who already
know it
too well
but she is drowned out
shouted down
by furious men
in sharply tailored suits
who insist that
what *they* have to say
is more valid
more important
more worthy
that what *she*
has to say

when called out
on their disrespectful
outburst
the men state

that they were
misunderstood
mischaracterized
'this would never
have happened'
they retort
'if others had
had simply obeyed
the RULES'

Composition of a Woman

Shrill: Notes from a Loud Woman

you call me *shrill*
loud
bitch
whenever I interrupt
whatever VERY important thing
you must be saying
to speak my truth
your tone patronizingly implying
that my voice is *so* shrill
it could break mirrors
etch glass
whenever I am audacious enough
to steal the floor from you
to speak
but why settle for merely etching glass
when I could engrave metal
chisel granite
write my truth onto the very stars?
maybe I am a shrill
loud bitch
you'll live

Christine E. Ray

What We're Told Not to Talk About

we liked you better
when you were a girl
with your mouth muzzled shut
by strong adult hands
seen but not heard
on your scabbed bony knees
easily rendered
docile
compliant

we liked you better
when you were young
held the shared secrets close
carried the blame
our blame
as if it were your own
eyes cast down
head hung in shame
feeling unclean
unheard
defeated

we liked you better
before something within you
started to wake
to stir
and you began clearing the debris

Composition of a Woman

painstakingly from your throat
with bare hands, knuckles bloody
looking up from the floor
to meet our gaze
simmering with mute rage
challenging our authority
our integrity

we liked you better
before you embraced your power
oiled the rust from your voice
with burning truth
rose slowly to your feet
to stand nose to nose
as you spoke at last
no longer tethered by shackles
we arrogantly thought
would hold you fast
a woman
defiant
empowered
her own

Christine E. Ray

We Should All Be Feminists

Feminist:*
adjective Sometimes fem·i·nis·tic.
advocating social, political, legal, and economic rights
for women equal to those of men.
noun an advocate of such rights.

I keep my feminist agenda
clearly displayed
on the refrigerator
whimsical magnets
holding it firmly in place
much to the discomfort
of those visitors
who are convinced
that feminists have no
sense of humor
I would like to say
that I cross items
off the list daily
but combatting toxic masculinity
eliminating outdated gender roles
stomping out rape culture
and smashing the patriarchy
are lifetime commitments
visitors are also flummoxed
to see my bra lying
on the stairs
perhaps they are surprised

Composition of a Woman

that a self-declared feminist
actually owns a bra
or perhaps they are
confusing me with
a stereotypical gay man
no one would *ever*
accuse me
of being tidy
my bra and I
have a love-hate relationship
or is it a
hate-hate relationship?
I hate the bra
but I hate the laws of gravity
even more
speaking of gay men
I think most people
really don't care
who puts what where
when two or more
consenting adults
are behind closed doors
I think homophobic men
are obsessed with the notion
that a man
attracted to
another man
could be perceived
as dainty
feminine

Christine E. Ray

dare I say?
womanly
we wouldn't want *that* now
would we?

*Dictionary.com

Composition of a Woman

Feminists Don't Wear Pink and Other Lies

feminism
the oxygen
I inhale gratefully
often desperately
in a world where
rapists' reputations
and futures
are held in higher regard
greater importance
than the legacy of trauma
inflicted upon girls
on women
against their will
where old white men
declare balls of dividing cells
have more rights
than living breathing women
reducing us to incubators
cows for milking
where I was seen
as two breasts
a womb
and a vagina
until I turned 50
and was suddenly
no longer visible at all
feminism is the iron
I pump into my veins
to replenish me
when I am bled dry
by the knowledge
of how many women

Christine E. Ray

chose a president like Trump
over their sisters
over themselves
some days
I wear black in mourning
Some days
I wear the red of resistance
and other days I even wear pink
in solidarity

Wonder Woman

the world needs me to be
Wonder Woman
but I keep thinking
that her outfit is ridiculous
I appreciate freedom of movement
as much as the next girl
and get the whole
aerodynamics thing
but really!?

I like my ass covered
and can we talk about those heels?!
give me a sturdy pair of Doc Martens
I need a costume
that is durable
tumble dry low
and has pockets
lots of pockets
because who can fight like that
with a purse slung around their neck?

I do like the lasso, though

all that red
white
and blue
seems awfully conspicuous

Christine E. Ray

and that gold lame?
completely impractical
unless I am trying to dazzle my enemies
I also think those wrist gauntlets
could be bigger and cooler
maybe Q could trick them out

the world needs me to be
Wonder Woman
but this depression
is seriously kicking my ass
what do the other
superheroes do
when it's hard to get out of bed
in the morning?
"Oh sorry, can't save the world today"!?

Batman could definitely
use an SSRI and some therapy
maybe 6 to 10 sessions of CBT
would do the trick
Superman is a little
too perfect for me
maybe he has a personality disorder
do you think there is a support group
for superheroes having
existential crises?
maybe I can run with Iron Man
I like his snark and he has cool toys

Composition of a Woman

the world needs me to be
Wonder Woman
I wish I felt more up to the task
guess it's time to put on my big girl pants
(the ones with all pockets)
take a deep breath
and get over myself
put out the call for
the other badass women out there
to grab their lassos
power up their invisible planes
there is humanity to save

Christine E. Ray

Black Roses and Moonlight

she brings black roses
and moonlight
fireflies like stars in her sky
bare feet caress the dewy ground
night blooming jasmine
reaching up to brush her opal skin
she is a casualty of time
forgotten midnight goddess slipped from her stem
name no longer invoked reverently on devout lips
her followers reduced to the night creatures who fly
above
trail at her feet
she shakes her head sadly at the sorry state of affairs
old ways replaced by franchised faith
found on televisions
drive-up chapels
where Elvis impersonators
listen to sins and dole out penance
under neon signs for just a small tithe
Visa, MasterCard and Discover accepted
they say you are what you worship
bemused she journeys on
wonders what humanity now prays for
in their concrete fortresses
surrounded by asphalt seas
something electronic perhaps. . .

Where the Mountain Meets the Moon

where the mountain
meets the moon
I shall stand
arms raised
in supplication
naked face lifted high
to be washed pure
by her silver glow
light shall
fill me
radiate out
from my deepest core
I will love
and be
beloved
embrace peace
and let it spill
from my soul
welcome myself
joyously
without judgment
and finally
become whole
where the mountain
meets the moon

Christine E. Ray

I Am the Woman

I am the Woman
your Mother warned you about
the one whose darkness
was hidden below the sunny faux finish
of excellent manners
honor roll grades
my monster heart hidden
so well that no one noticed
me drowning
in my self-hate
I am the Woman
who cut my teeth
on black leather
and handcuffs
control a requirement
for my release
I am the Woman
with scrolls of black ink
symbols of resistance
of resilience
etched inch by inch
on my skin
a reclaiming of a body
that was not always
my home
I am the Woman
who casually mentions

Composition of a Woman

my ex-lovers
male and female
at the holiday table
pass the gravy please
I am the Woman
who finally started to speak
silence is *not* golden
truth is silver
and has wings

Christine E. Ray

The Sins of My Father

I have always been a dreamer. Waking hours filled with daydreams of a younger, more vibrant me living other, more exotic lives that take the edge off the stupor of middle-age suburbia. Sleeping hours filled with images of places I have been before that morph and change, nightmarish Wonderlands, and places I have never been that haunt me just the same. Some nights I languish in cages built of my rigid small town girlhood; other nights I am prey climbing out of impossibly small, high windows, crawling through rough stone tunnels, hiding behind faux fireplaces on the run for my life. Or at least for my freedom.

Some dreams find me on my knees, lips and tongue forming the shape of silent prayers, fingers anxiously reading the silver chains that confine me like a blind woman's rosary. My waking self is a recovered Catholic who rarely walks through the doors of a church willingly. In solitary rebellion, I refuse to kneel and sing loudly to myself to drown out the traitor chorus of "Our Fathers," "Hail Marys," and "Amens" that play in my head. They are etched more deeply into my impressionable neurons than high school calculus or chemistry ever were.

I envision a grim future where I will forget my deep distrust of organized religion but my muscles will still remember how to genuflect like the most devout of

Composition of a Woman

believers. It strikes me as cruelly ironic that dementia may one day steal my lifelong oppositional defiance but that the empty rituals of Catholicism will never die. I have always suspected the Christian-Judeo God of being a wily bastard, always needing to have the last word.

The shadow filled rooms are always too cold, the kneeler cushions too thin and covered in grit. Debris digs into my bare skin, leaving odd-shaped impressions, Rorschachs of sin to be interpreted at another time. Frankincense and myrrh a miasma of smoke that makes my eyes tear, my throat itch.

It is never clear to me who I am praying to. Have I made peace with a monotheistic god in these dreams or do the Goddess and Green Man listen to my entreats? What I am praying for is also a mystery. I only know that I bow my head in atonement.

Mea culpa
Mea Culpa
Maxima Culpa

That Was Then, This Is Now

I used to worry that others
would finally see the truth of me
my midnight darkness
entwined with silver light
reject me as the monster
withdraw their love
threaten to set my house ablaze
with their self-righteous torches
I no longer have the time
nor the patience
for the faint of heart
the weak of will
I will not change
or contort myself
to earn the thin gruel
of such conditional love
I was made for bigger dreams
fiercer souls

Composition of a Woman

Lilith

you look at my nakedness
and call me 'Eve'
name my sins
disobedience
greed
as you take the apple willingly
from my hand
but I am no Eve
offering temptation of the tree of knowledge's sweet fruit
serpent wrapped around the branch above my head

I am Lilith
the first
shaped of the same dirt
as Adam
so the legend goes
I am not of dirt
but of fire
his equal
unbending
headstrong
refusing to lie beneath him
in supplication

society names my sin
calls me
whore

Christine E. Ray

temptress
sorceress
demon
accuses me of
vexing the sons of men
with lustful dreams
leading them to defile themselves
as though it matters to me
where their seed is spilled

I will travel the ancient ways
clothed only in my dark tresses
my alabaster skin
don a crown of rose and poppy
their scent filling the air
I will take back this night
shape its darkness with my hands
make it blaze with stars and moonlight
create a road for my daughters and sisters
to follow home

Indigo

stripped down
to ink
to bone
I am revealed
surplus marble
carved away
leaving deep
curves
razor sharp
edges
baptized
by neon lights
bathed in
sacred
indigo glow
I am the night
I am the night
I am the night

Christine E. Ray

Raven

it starts as tightness
tingling
across bare shoulder blades
becomes an itch
I can't quite reach
stretch my spine sinuous
slow
vertebrae by vertebrae
long for a shot of whiskey
or three
liquid gold disinhibition I can blame
for the reckless choice
I am about to make
I finally let go
tightly coiled control
gasp with relief
as I finally unleash the darkness
onyx feathers rip
sharp and true through the flesh of my back
talons shoot from fingertips
toes
bones burned hollow
by demon fire dwelling in my belly
exquisite pain of rebirth
brings me briefly to my knees
I arise something new
wipe the blood from my mouth

Composition of a Woman

spread fledgling wings
and with the lift of the north wind
I claim the night sky
mine

Christine E. Ray

When God Was a Woman

Sunday morning sermons
delivered from man-made pulpits
echo in our ears
his-story books
that line school shelves
providing the warp
the weft
that weave the elaborate
mythic tapestry
a master-piece of
collective amnesia
millenniums in the making
a palatable image
to hang on our walls
of an all-knowing, all-powerful
thunderous God
his pristine ivory robes
rustling gracefully
over his magnificent manhood
a white-washed God
for the masses to fear
to revere
to swallow whole
with their bitter
communion wine
we are the women
who remember

Composition of a Woman

when God was a woman
when the earth gestated
and flourished
in her cosmic womb
supported by her strong brown hands
we are the women
who will not forget
who teach our daughters
the old ways in secret parlors
sandy beaches
fertile fields
who guide their arms lovingly
in gratitude to the full moon
stars shining brightly
on their tender brows
a crown
her truth burning brightly
in their hearts

Christine E. Ray

We Are the Witches

'We are the granddaughters of the witches they weren't able to burn.'
Tish Thawer

the god-fearing men
who wish to tie us
to stakes
sew lions on their standards
to give them courage
play at soldier
like little boys
carrying pointy sticks
and bibles
in their self-righteous hands
hypocrites
who lust for the maiden
revere the mother
deathly fear the crone
we are all faces
of the triple goddess
we worship her
by the light of the moon
we are the witches
the keepers of wisdom
who pass down the lore
of our foremothers
we remember

Composition of a Woman

and honor
the magic in the earth
the power in our blood
granddaughters
of the women
your grandfathers
could not burn

Christine E. Ray

What Makes a Woman

no lipstick
sits upon my dresser top
no long-handled brush
graces my hair
for 100 nightly strokes
bras
panties
nestle neatly
in the upper drawer
in practical cottons
not a bow
or piece of lace
to be found
faint lines around the eyes
silver threaded through
close-cropped hair
betray my age
but do not give away
my tempestuous heart
beating beneath
today's ironic tee
or my siren soul
that sings
French torch songs
softly to myself
I know that you are
blinded by my

Composition of a Woman

middle-age
tomboy appearance
but passion
longing
are still
a fathomless well
inside my breast

Christine E. Ray

Seed

they tell me
I am no longer
a bringer of life
since monthly ruby tides
synced to moon rhythms
have ceased
they call me
desiccated
crone
barren
obsolete
they do not know
my truth
my womb
my soul
primordial oceans
humming with
single cell organisms
itching to divide
multiply
to explode with
fecund creativity
feminine power
waiting taut
to be unleashed
with passion
with fury

Composition of a Woman

recreate this universe
in *her* image
realign the stars
this is why the world
of men
in the armor of their three piece suits
and patronizing voices
fear the sexuality
of middle age women
orgasmic contractions
of our womb
acid words from our pens
our combined voices
a hail of silver bullets disrupting
the smoke of illusion
shattering the mirrors
of status quo

Christine E. Ray

Stepping Off the Spiral Path

no longer virginal maiden
lips like ripe peach
no longer fertile earth mother
babe at breast
I have fallen out of memory
fallen out of myth
filled with the wisdom
of time
experience
I reject the title *crone*
I am decades from being wise woman
alone in the woods
is there no place
on the spiral of life
in a society obsessed with youth
beauty
for a midlife woman
come into her own
comfortable in her own skin
in her own sexuality
sharp of mind
no longer defined solely
by relationships to others?
my vibrancy undimmed
my ambition awakened
I refuse the mantle
of invisibility

Composition of a Woman

only sanctioned option offered me
I choose instead my naked soul
blaze my own trail
in a world unprepared for smart
passionate
confident
hungry women
who do not fit in a rigid mold
who belong solely
to themselves

Christine E. Ray

This Bridge Called My Back

young ones
you glance
in my direction
but you do not see
your eyes slide off me
as if I wear my gray hair
my fine lines
like a woven cloak
of invisibility
should I strip myself
in front of you
baring my vulnerability
baring my rage?
could you then see
what lies beneath?
this bridge
called my back
anchored with bone
cabled with nerve
built on a foundation
of blood
and tears
calcium phosphate
and pain
arched with collagen
and passion
has carried the weight

Composition of a Woman

of mothers
has carried the weight
of daughters
has lifted you higher
than I was taught
to dream
your toes dug deeply
into my ribs
as you pulled yourself up
on my shoulders
and the shoulders
of my sisters
history might forget us
but the bridges
of our backs
will remain

Christine E. Ray

In Search of Our Mother's Gardens

dear mother
you hid your heart
behind stone walls
and locked gates
a secret garden
you never invited me
into for tea
glimpses of daisies
black-eyes susans
lily of the valley
stolen through
cast iron posts
while standing on
tippy-toe
dear grandmother
you gave your love
more easily
my constant gardener
tending to hearth
to home
your summer arms filled
with purple and white lilacs
large blooms of hydrangea
the air around you
fragrant with wisteria
I have planted a garden
of a different kind

Composition of a Woman

syllables and words
buried deep in the rich soil
of wistfulness
and loss
memory
and longing
I have gradually cut back the
overgrowth
allowing sunlight
and a generous watering of tears
to bathe the seedlings
in hopes that my children
will reap their own truths
from all that we have sown

Christine E. Ray

Lost Voice

siren's golden voice
once dropped confident syllables
into air
as naturally as breathing
now stifled in constricted throat
that struggles to swallow
six-sided anxiety
hot, sour bile
college ruled notebooks
once full
of manic scribblings
compulsively captured in black ink
before inspiration could swirl down the floor drain
collect dust
sigh from disuse
pen now held in death grip
fingers have lost their grace
their nerve
fertile mind now an empty room
where silence rings
torturous tinnitus
blindfolded by fear
weight pressing down on shoulders
by the weight of giant
unseen inquisitor's voice barks
Have you reached the bottom of yourself
are you so shallow

Composition of a Woman

so barren?!
Or is truth so deeply hidden
that you must dive inside
hand to elbow buried into slippery entrails
to reach it?
surgical implements laid out
with precision on a stainless tray
slide into view
no hesitation picking up sharp scalpel
with shaking fingers
a writer's way is
always to bleed

I Want To Fall In Love Again

I want to fall
in love
with words
again
roll them
sensuously
around my mouth
caress them slowly
with teeth
with tongue
before I swallow
whole
their rich taste
of chocolate
and bourbon
a silken burn
as they work
their way
slowly down
to my core
I want to fall
in love
with sentences
again
that coalesce
within my veins
feel them thrum

Composition of a Woman

electric
in my blood
with each beat
of this poet's heart
I want to fall
in love
again
with virgin
parchment
that sits
forlornly
upon my desk
longing to be filled
after inking my pen
deep crimson red
spilling my
sacred truth

Christine E. Ray

Woman Seeking Poetry

I am looking
for poetry
in everyday
objects
the story
unfolding
in the pulse
of a day
I am looking
for beauty
in the moth
on my
fingertip
the music
of spring breezes
mussing my hair
I am seeking
the place
at the core
of my soul
where words
used to
glitter
like fine grains
of sand
on the banks
of my shore

Composition of a Woman

I Am

I am
fragments of poetry
wisps of dreams
drifting musical notes
memories captured in amber
metal dragons
origami cranes
blood orange kisses
words of strength
etched in ink on skin

poet's soul
woman's heart
lover's passion
witch's spirit
shield maiden's battle cry
pieces of me, all

I drink the moon
hear my own music in my veins
listen to all the women I am
who demand to be
made visible
made whole

who tell me that I am
done apologizing

Christine E. Ray

done containing
my darkness
my fierceness
my light
to make others comfortable

I am
done whispering

Poet's Love Song

I see you
yes, you poet
you who lives
behind the misty veil
dwelling in the border
between this world
and a hundred other
shadow worlds

I *see* you

I *see* those ink-stained
fingers
that hold your pen
like a lover
that fly across the keyboard
in a torrent
before stopping, hesitating
waiting
for the flow of words to resume

I *see* the permanent rings
countless cups of coffee
have left on your writing table
the chip in your favorite mug
I see the frayed fabric
on your cuffs

of your favorite writing shirt
the fabric worn thin at your elbows

I *see* those mesmerizing eyes
that seem to simultaneously
be looking through me
straight into my soul
while studying the cosmos
and gazing inward
all at the same time
I *see* the contradictions you are
your eyes are haunting
full of knowing
full of pain
full of longing

I *see* the dark smudges
under your otherworldly eyes
reminders that poets
are night dwellers
insomniacs
who haunt the still hours
who understand the depth
the texture of darkness
who can capture the qualities
the acoustics of silence

I *see* the way
words spill out of
your sensuous mouth

Composition of a Woman

like pearls, like diamonds
beautiful treasures
embedded with your tears
your sweat, your blood

yes poet
I *see* you
you who makes me fall
in love with language
over and over
whose words
stab me in the heart
punch me in the gut
jangle my nerves
bathe me in your radiance
soothe my weary soul
take me on a journey
I didn't even know
I wanted to go on

and *you* are beautiful

Christine E. Ray

On Becoming a Poet

sometimes, adopting the names 'writer' and 'poet'
led her to encounters with the most amazing minds
connecting her with a larger community
at other times she thought that 'writer' and 'poet'
were the loneliest names she had ever called herself
waking up every morning
to unzip her chest, her gut
and bare her truths to the world
because like others of her kind
she was complex, messy, containing
multiple truths, not a singular one

sometimes she felt like she was writing
to a small group of intimate friends
at others times
she felt like she was calling out her truths
into an empty desert landscape
without even a coyote or armadillo
to hear her words before they fell away
forlorn and unread
unheard and unacknowledged
rendering the writer, the poet herself
invisible, diminished somehow

she was always struck by the juxtaposition
of her physical body negotiating
close suburbs

Composition of a Woman

crowded subways and jostling city sidewalks
on the way to her day job
while her heart and mind
wandered in the isolated wilderness
while errant words and wisps of dreams
and drops of feelings like rich, red blood
continued to seep out of her

About the Author

Christine E. Ray is an author, editor, and micro-publisher from the Greater Philadelphia area, Pennsylvania, USA. Her debut collection of poetry *Composition of Woman* was published in July 2018 by Sudden Denouement Publishing. It became a 2019 Reader's Favorite Bronze Medal winner in Poetry. Her second collection of poetry *The Myths of Girlhood* was released by Indie Blu(e) Publishing in January of 2019.

Ray's writing has been featured in SpillWords, fēlan poetry & visual zine, Nicholas Gagnier's *Swear to Me* (2017), as well as Gagnier's *All the Lonely People* (2019). She also contributed to and served as an editor for *Anthology Volume I: Writings from the Sudden Denouement Literary Collective* (2018) and *We Will Not Be Silenced: The Lived Experience of Sexual Harassment and Sexual Assault Told Powerfully Through Poetry, Essay, and Art*.

www.ingramcontent.com/pod-product-compliance
Lightning Source LLC
Chambersburg PA
CBHW020410080526
44584CB00014B/1259